ESSENTIAL KEYBOARD TRIOS

10 INTERMEDIATE TO EARLY ADVANCED SELECTIONS

IN THEIR ORIGINAL FORM

 SELECTED AND EDITED BY
LUCY MAURO AND SCOTT BEARD

Cover art: Confidences
by Cristiano Banti (Italian, 1824–1904)
Galleria d'Arte Moderna, Florence, Italy
The Bridgeman Art Library

ISBN-10: 0-7390-4534-2
ISBN-13: 978-0-7390-4534-3

ESSENTIAL KEYBOARD TRIOS
Music for Six Hands, One Piano
10 Intermediate to Early Advanced Selections
in Their Original Form

Selected and Edited by Lucy Mauro and Scott Beard

Historical Background

Keyboard trios (music for six hands at one piano) have been a unique part of piano ensemble repertoire for the past 150 years. Works for three players at separate keyboards can be found in the 17th and 18th centuries, such as an untitled piece for three organs by Pietro Della Valle (1586–1652), concertos for three harpsichords by Johann Sebastian Bach (1685–1750) and the "Lodron" concerto by Wolfgang Amadeus Mozart (1756–1791). However, it was in the early 19th century—with the development of the piano and larger instruments—that compositions for six hands at one keyboard began to appear in the form of both original compositions and arrangements of popular works.

As with many piano duets, teachers often composed six-hand pieces for their pupils. Some of the earliest composers of six-hand music include Wilhelm Friedrich Ernst Bach (1759–1845), Joseph Mazzinghi (1765–1844), Carolus Antonius Fodor (1768–1846) and Carl Czerny (1791–1857).

In the 19th century, *salon* works for six hands gained in popularity, and by the early 20th century, the educational value of this ensemble became widely recognized by teachers, pedagogical composers and publishers alike. Many compositions from this period carry subtitles such as "The Three Sisters" or the "The Three Amateurs," reflecting ensemble playing in the home with friends and family. Today, six-hand works are included in private and group lessons, with new compositions and arrangements being published regularly.

In addition to its pedagogical use, the six-hand medium has occasionally found a place on the contemporary concert stage, with works such as Noël Lee's *Pret à partir* and *Trois sur un clavier*, Peter Schickele's *Chapbook* and passages from George Crumb's *Celestial Mechanics*.

About This Collection

To facilitate reading, the pieces in this collection are presented in score form, which enables each player to see all the parts. Fingerings, redistributions and all parenthetical material are editorial. Ornaments are realized in footnotes at their initial appearance in each work. Performers are encouraged to experiment with additional ornamentation and other realizations as appropriate to the work's style and level of the players.

Pedaling is left to the discretion of the performers. Footnotes indicate the few instances where the composer's original pedal markings appear. Final pedaling decisions should be based on a number of factors, including style, balance, musical intentions, the level of the performers, the actual instrument and the performance environment (acoustics).

Balance is one of the most important elements in six-hand playing. While some composers suggest a louder dynamic for the most prominent part, others indicate the same dynamic level for all three parts. Performers will need to be aware of the featured melodic material and how the dynamics in all three parts relate to each other.

Performance Suggestions

Three performers playing at one keyboard requires special consideration with regard to seating positions. Individual adjustable benches work well and may be positioned with the narrow sides of the benches facing the keyboard, with the two outer benches placed at a slight angle. This allows for individual height and distance adjustment, and also provides somewhat more room than the traditional placement of the benches. In the absence of adjustable benches, side chairs may be used, or even a combination of side chairs and a traditional bench. Each player will need to find his or her comfortable position and, most importantly, maintain that seating position when practicing alone.

When performing six-hand works, careful attention is required for finger and hand placement on the keyboard. In general, each player is confined to a specific range on the piano. Occasionally, performers will need to exchange notes quickly, or fingers and hands may overlap. The editors have added footnotes to address passages where players' hands must cross.

Pedaling also requires special considerations in six-hand performance. Because of the proximity to the pedal, the *secondo* player usually performs the pedaling. In some instances, pedaling could be shared by the players. For example, the *terzo* player may use the *una corda* pedal while the *secondo* manages the damper pedal. In any event, good ensemble playing requires that pedaling decisions be made well in advance of the performance, and any special pedal usage should be marked clearly on the score.

To help students distinguish their individual part quickly while reading in score form, it may be helpful to highlight—in different colors—the roman numerals at the beginning of each system for the first (*primo*), second (*secondo*) and third (*terzo*) parts.

Two final considerations for this type of ensemble playing are cueing and page turning. Performers need to decide which player will be responsible for discreetly gesturing beginnings, endings and other important points of phrasing. For secure performances, cues and page-turning designations should be clearly labeled on the score.

Pedagogical Value

Keyboard trios are not only an enjoyable and entertaining form of ensemble music, but also an effective medium for building musicianship and ensemble-playing skills. Six-hand music develops listening skills, technique, rhythmic control and score-reading abilities. This type of ensemble playing also builds a sense of teamwork and leadership skills. Teachers have many possibilities for forming keyboard trios in their studio, including combining friends, siblings or other family members, or students of various ages and levels of advancement. The works in this collection make excellent recital pieces, as performers and audiences alike enjoy the unique musical experience of six hands at one piano.

Suggested Reading

Bigler, Carole and Valerie Lloyd-Watts. *Ornamentation: A Question & Answer Manual.* Van Nuys, CA: Alfred Publishing Co., Inc., 1995.

Maxwell, Grant L. *Music for Three or More Pianists: A Historical Survey and Catalogue.* Metuchen, NJ: The Scarecrow Press, Inc., 1993.

Contents Listed by Composer

Bolero

Jean Louis Streabbog
(1835–1886)

6

(a) Play the grace note almost simultaneously with the main note.

Das Dreyblatt

Wilhelm Friedrich Ernst Bach
(1759–1845)

Andante con moto
For hand positions, see About the Composers and the Music (p. 139)

(a) Play the grace note almost simultaneously with the main note.

(c) Play an unmeasured trill beginning on the upper note.

(b)

(d)

(e) Play an unmeasured trill beginning on the main note.

12

ⓗ ⓘ ⓙ Play the grace note almost simultaneously with the main note.

(k) Play the grace notes slightly before the beat.

14

Ⓜ Play the grace notes slightly before the beat.

(n) Optional cadenza by Lucy Mauro. If omitting the cadenza, skip to beat 2 of measure 55.

⊙ A slight stress on the first "A" (*primo*) and the first "F" (*terzo*) will help ensemble precision.

20

ⓡ For this challenging passage, the *primo* should play at the back of the keys, towards the fallboard, and the *terzo* at the front.

Avanzando

(s) *Primo* may play the downbeat "A" of the *terzo* part.

(t) Play an unmeasured trill beginning on the main notes.

Hallelujah Chorus
from *Messiah*

George Frideric Handel (1685–1759)
Arr. by Carl Czerny (1791–1857)

ⓐ Play an unmeasured trill beginning on the upper note.

(b) Play an unmeasured trill beginning on the upper note.

32

ⓒ ⓓ Play an unmeasured trill beginning on the upper note.

OVERTURE
from *The Marriage of Figaro*

Wolfgang A. Mozart (1756–1791)
Arr. by Carl Czerny (1791–1857)

ⓐ Pedal indication is by Czerny.

ⓑ ⓒ Play the grace notes on the beat.

44

ⓓ Play an unmeasured trill beginning on the upper (grace) note.

46

48

ⓔ Play an unmeasured trill beginning on the main note.

50

Ⓕ Play an unmeasured trill beginning on the upper (grace) note.

(g) Possible redistribution for the *secondo* part: take the fourth eighth note (D) with the left hand.

(h) Play an unmeasured trill beginning on the main note.

VALSE

Sergei Rachmaninoff
(1873–1943)

ⓐ ⓑ The *secondo* LH plays over the *terzo* RH.

© Play the lower A as a grace note before the beat.

68

ROMANCE

Sergei Rachmaninoff
(1873–1943)

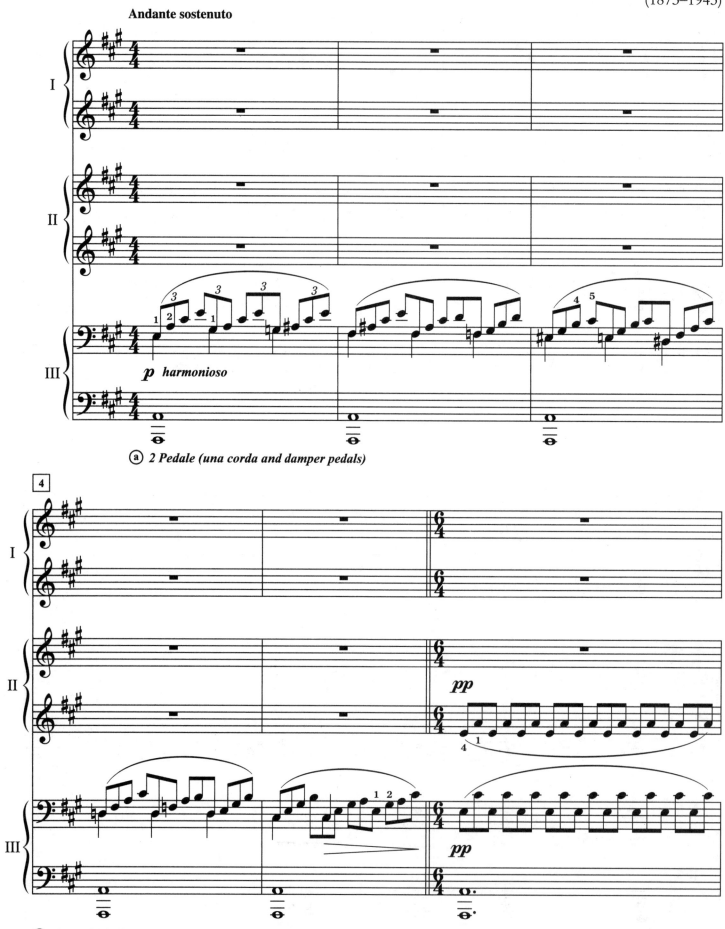

ⓐ 2 Pedale (una corda and damper pedals)

ⓐ The pedal indications in measures 1, 34 and 47 are the composer's.

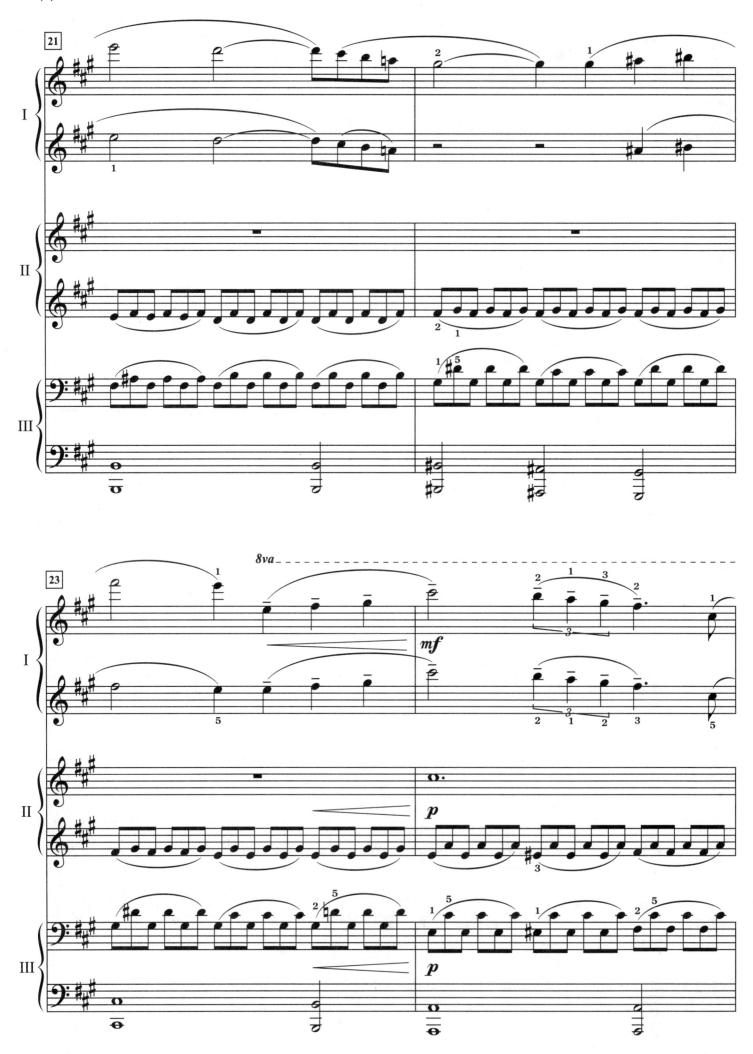

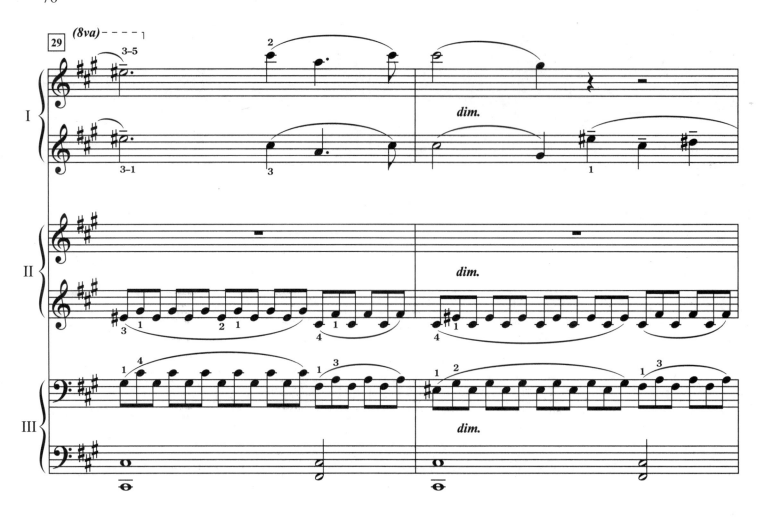

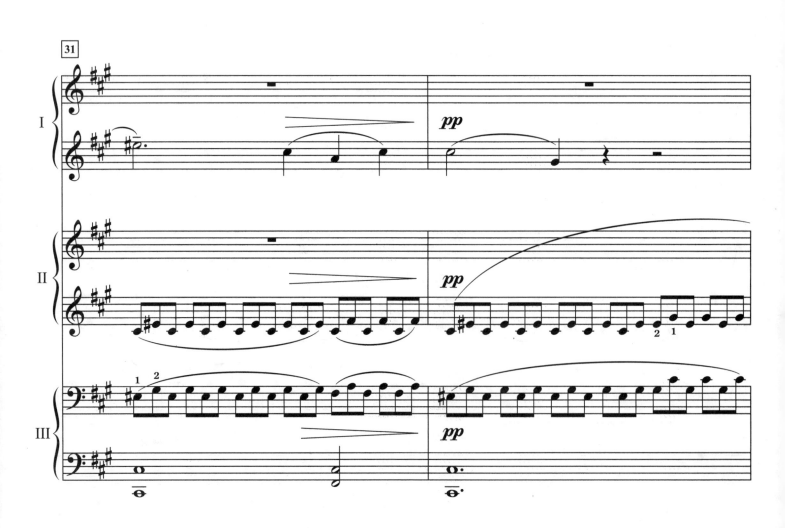

ⓑ ⓒ The *secondo* LH plays over the *terzo* RH.

una corda (sin' al fine) (soft pedal until the end)

SONATA FOR SIX HANDS

Carolus Antonius Fodor (1768–1846)
Op. 10

⓫ or an unmeasured trill beginning on the upper note.

ⓒ Play an unmeasured trill beginning on the upper note.

RONDO

ⓐ Dynamics are editorial.

ⓑⓒ Play the grace note almost simultaneously with the main note.

ⓓ Play the grace note almost simultaneously with the main note.

GAVOTTA

Cornelius Gurlitt (1820–1901)
Op. 192, No. 2

IMPROMPTU

Cornelius Gurlitt (1820–1901)
Op. 192, No. 6

(a) Play the grace note almost simultaneously with the main note.

122

(b) Play an unmeasured trill beginning on the main note.

124

CAPRICCIETTA

Cornelius Gurlitt (1820–1901)
Op. 192, No. 3

134

About the Composers and the Music

Wilhelm Friedrich Ernst Bach (1759–1845) was the grandson of Johann Sebastian Bach (1685–1750) and the son of Johann Christoph Friedrich Bach (1732–1795). He gained some measure of fame as a composer during his lifetime, and his long life allowed him to meet both Robert Schumann (1810–1856) and Felix Mendelssohn (1809–1847). W. F. E. Bach served as *Kapellmeister* and keyboard teacher in Berlin for Queen Elisabeth Christine and later as music instructor for Queen Luise. His numerous compositions include vocal, keyboard, orchestral and chamber works.

Das Dreyblatt is a charming piece that takes its title ("The Trefoil") from the three-leafed image. The work reflects the influence of the Classical style as well as Bach's sense of humor, as he suggests that the *secondo* pianist be a man amid two women playing the *primo* and *terzo* parts, crossing arms throughout the piece. Cameron McGraw, in his book *Piano Duet Repertoire* (Indiana University Press, 1981), includes the following translation of Bach's performance instructions:

> The gentleman playing in the middle part should sit a little further back than the two ladies on either side of him. Their arms should be held above his own. The restricted space makes it necessary for the three performers to sit somewhat closely together, the man in the middle playing the highest notes with his right hand, and the lowest notes with his left.

Carl Czerny (1791–1857) was an Austrian composer, pianist and teacher. A prolific composer, he published more than 1,000 compositions during his lifetime. He is largely known today for his outstanding collections of technical studies such as *The School of Velocity* and *The Art of Finger Dexterity*. A dedicated teacher, Czerny taught some of the most influential pianists of the 19th century including Franz Liszt (1811–1886) and Theodor Leschetizky (1830–1915).

Czerny was one of the first composers to write a significant amount of music for keyboard trio. His arrangement of the "Hallelujah Chorus" (from *Messiah* by George Frideric Handel, 1685-1759) comes from a set of *Rondinos*, Op. 609 that includes the subtitle "The Three Sisters." Other works in the set include *Air Suisse: Lullaby* and an arrangement of *Rule Britannia*. Czerny also made arrangements for six hands of several opera overtures, including Mozart's *Don Giovanni*, Rossini's *Tancredi* and Weber's *Der Freischütz*. His arrangement of Mozart's overture to *Le nozze di Figaro (The Marriage of Figaro)* is one of the most challenging and exciting works in the six-hand literature.

Carolus Antonius Fodor (1768–1846) was a Dutch composer, conductor and pianist who came from a distinguished musical family. His brother Josephus Andreas was a virtuoso violinist, his brother Carolus Emanuel was a well-known harpichordist who immigrated to France, and his niece Joséphine Fodor-Mainvielle was an acclaimed operatic soprano. Carolus Antonius was a prominent conductor in Amsterdam and a noted composer whose numerous works include piano concertos, symphonies, cantatas and chamber pieces.

The *Sonata for Six Hands*, Op. 10 is one of the first original sonatas for three players at one keyboard. The work, which was published circa 1800, shows Fodor's skill at writing for this emerging medium. Both movements contain many points of imitation, with material that is cleverly divided among the three players.

Cornelius Gurlitt (1820–1901) was a German composer, pianist and organist. He was a student of J. P. Rudolf Reinecke, the father of composer Carl Reinecke (1824–1910). Early in his career, Gurlitt traveled throughout Europe, meeting Robert Schumann, Robert Franz and other prominent musicians. Although he composed operas, cantatas and symphonies, Gurlitt is best known today for his well-crafted and appealing pedagogical works for the piano.

Gavotta, Capriccietta and *Impromptu* from *Six Pieces*, Op. 192 are Romantic character pieces written in ternary form (**A B A**). With all three parts generally equal in difficulty, these works make a good introduction to six-hand playing at the intermediate level. *Gavotta*, the second work of the set, shows the inspiration of the French folk dance. While Gurlitt uses a $\frac{4}{4}$ meter, the character of the dance—which is typically in duple meter—may be best felt with a pulse of two beats per measure. *Capriccietta*, literally a "little whim or fancy," is reminiscent of Baroque keyboard writing with its contrapuntal passages and short points of imitation. With *Impromptu*, the final work of the set, Gurlitt creates a sense of drama with the use of the minor key, a syncopated melody and improvisatory-like passagework.

George Frideric Handel (1685–1759) was one of the greatest composers of the Baroque period. Born in Germany, he settled in England where he became a leading composer of both vocal and instrumental works. Handel resided in England for over 45 years and is buried in Westminster Abbey. He is particularly renowned for his oratorios—large-scale vocal works that are religious in nature, containing musical elements of opera (overture, recitatives, arias and choruses), but without staging.

The "Hallelujah Chorus" is one of the most well-known and beloved pieces in classical music. The chorus closes Part II of Handel's three-part oratorio, *Messiah*. The oratorio, which has a text adapted by Charles Jennens, was premiered in Dublin in 1742 to great acclaim and has since become one of the most frequently performed pieces of classical literature.

Wolfgang Amadeus Mozart (1756–1791) is regarded as one of the greatest composers and musical talents of all time. Born in Austria, he received his early musical training from his father Leopold (1719–1787), a respected musician. Leopold Mozart recognized his son's exceptional talent and took the young Mozart and his sister Maria Anna ("Nannerl") on frequent concert tours throughout Europe. Mozart's mature compositions, such as *The Marriage of Figaro*, represent the height of the Viennese Classical style.

The Marriage of Figaro, an *opera buffa* (comic opera), is the first of three operas by Mozart with a libretto by Lorenzo Da Ponte (1749–1838). The opera is based on the play *La folle journée ou Le mariage de Figaro* ("The Crazy Day or The Marriage of Figaro") by Beaumarchais (1732–1799), a witty story of love, revenge and mistaken identity. In the opera's brilliant overture—which does not draw on themes from the opera itself—Mozart uses exciting passagework, a *presto* tempo and triumphant chordal passages to set the mood for the lively action that is to follow.

Sergei Rachmaninoff (1873–1943) was a Russian pianist and composer, widely recognized as one of the greatest pianists of the 20th century. Rachmaninoff's compositions are known for their extraordinary beauty, lyricism and uniquely colorful late-Romantic style. His *Preludes*, Op. 23 and Op. 32, *Etudes-tableaux*, *Piano Concerto No. 2 in C Minor*, and the *Piano Concerto No. 3 in D Minor* are heard every season in major concert venues throughout the world. Rachmaninoff became a permanent resident of the United States in 1917 and remained in America until his death in Beverly Hills, California in 1943.

Valse and *Romance* date from 1890 and 1891 respectively, and were composed for three sisters who were Rachmaninoff's cousins: Natalya, Lyudmila and Vera Skalon. In both pieces, glimpses of Rachmaninoff's mature style can be heard in the chromatic melodies and harmonies, and use of colorful registers of the piano. *Valse* is in the lighter style of a *salon* piece. Rachmaninoff uses melodic material in all three parts. *Romance*, as the title suggests, is a more dramatic work. Rachmaninoff would later use the opening material of this work in the second movement of his *Piano Concerto No. 2*. Ruth Burgess, in a 1960 edition of *Romance* (Leeds Music), included the following translation of the young Rachmaninoff's directions, which he sent to the Skalon sisters:

> This piece should be performed not too fast. Better to play it slowly and almost entirely with the second pedal. The melody and harmony should stand out. In the beginning, the Primo part should stand out. On the other hand, at the beginning of the middle section, the Primo should be subordinate to the Terzo part. I do not envy, from my point of view, the performer of the Secondo part—this part constantly has the accompaniment and further more, always plays "piano." My advice to the dear performers: first study each part separately. After studying it as necessary, play the piece together. I ask you to please follow my advice, otherwise, in my opinion, nothing will come out.

Jean Louis Streabbog (1835–1886) was a Belgian pianist and composer. He published under the pseudonym Streabbog, which is his original name, Gobbaerts, spelled backwards. Streabogg was a prolific composer whose works are typically written in a lighter *salon* style. Today, he is largely remembered for his pedagogical pieces, many of which were written for the intermediate piano student.

A *bolero* is a Spanish dance in triple meter that may also include vocal lines and subtle percussion effects. Streabbog captures the spirited quality of the dance in this *Bolero* by using repeated notes and chords, as well as descending triplet figures in the melodic line. Written in ternary form (**A B A**), the lyrical middle section in C major recalls a serenade, and an exact return of the **A** section, in A minor, closes the work.